Children's Book of Yoga

Children's Book of Yoga

Games & Exercises Mimic
Plants & Animals & Objects

THIA LUBY

CLEAR LIGHT PUBLISHERS
SANTA FE, NEW MEXICO

DEDICATION

This book is dedicated to my parents, who were both teachers and inspired me to lead my life in the direction of offering my interests and knowledge to everyone around me ...sharing my love of yoga with the world.

© 1998 Text and Photos by Thia Luby.
Additional Photo Credits:
Animals Animals © David M. Barron, page 40; © Patti Murray, page 44.
Cholla Earth Scenes: © Donna Ikenberry, page 28
Bruce Coleman, Inc.: © Norman Tomalin, page 66; © Jeff Foott, page 94;
© Peter Ward, page 98
© Marcia Keegan, pages 14, 26, 60
Photo Researchers, Inc.: © John Chumack; E. Hanumantha Rao, pages 2, 56; © Francis Gohier, page 102
Wildlife Collection: © D. Robert Franz
Photo Researcher: Eva Tucholka

Clear Light Publishers
823 Don Diego, Santa Fe, NM 87501
WEB: www.clearlightbooks.com

First Edition
10 9 8 7 6 5 4

LIBRARY OF CONGRESS CATALOGING-IN-PUBLICATION DATA

Luby, Thia, 1954–
    Children's book of yoga: games & exercises mimic plants & animals & objects / Thia Luby.
        p. cm.
    Summary: Presents six complete yoga workouts designed for children from three to twelve years of age.
    ISBN 1-57416-003-6 (cloth)
    1. Yoga, Hatha—Juvenile literature. 2. Exercise—Juvenile literature. 3. Yoga, Hatha, for children—Juvenile literature. 4. Exercise for children—Juvenile literature. [1. Yoga.]
RA781.7.L814   1998
613.7'046—dc21

98-9712
CIP
AC

The publisher and author accept no responsibility or liability for injuries that may result from use of the information in this book. Readers are expected to follow recommended precautions and make allowances for differences in children's abilities and physical condition.

Printed in Hong Kong

Acknowledgments

Many thanks to the children who
participated in this book, along with their parents.

Madeleine Aguilar

Chris Bonifer

Matt Bonifer

Stephany Bonifer

Shelby Hilgerdt-Bovee

Ariana Cohen

David Cohen

Ariel Gudwin

Sofia Kraft

Misty Myers

Theo Newhall

Molly Norton

Skylar Rote

Weston Settegast

Sarah Spier

Teague Stroh

Joseph Turner

Adrianna Yoder

August Young

Page Young

Contents

Yoga for Children

What Is Yoga?

The word "yoga" means "union." Developed in India over 5,000 years ago, yoga is an ancient science that teaches the importance of allowing the mind and body to unite and work in harmony for the creation of a more balanced, responsible human being. It is a system of health combining vast numbers of exercises or poses that keep the body and mind working together to build strength, flexibility, balance, and concentration. These poses imitate things in our environment like animals or objects. By learning to imitate things with the body, we are opening the mind to new levels of understanding body awareness and building self-esteem.

This unique health practice is becoming more and more popular in the United States as more people learn the benefits of this ancient healing art. It is designed to keep the internal organs healthy along with strengthening muscles and bones, and increasing flexibility of joints, tendons, and ligaments. By holding poses, the blood works into different parts of the body to stimulate organs or open blocked passageways.

There are four categories of poses to practice: seated, standing, lying down, and upside down. Within each category there are backward bends, twists, and forward bends. Each pose gives numerous benefits. There are so many different variations on poses to practice, you can never be bored in yoga! Constant practice brings new discoveries and is eternally enlightening.

Why Should Children Do Yoga?

This book contains valuable, fun information on how children ages 3 to 12 can enjoy the benefits of learning a variety of yoga poses by imitating animals or objects in the environment, along with learning new ways to develop deep, healthful breathing. Classic yoga poses are presented in this book together with original poses and games created by the author. (The author's original games and poses are marked with an asterisk in the lists of poses at the back of the book.) A few classic poses have been renamed or otherwise adapted for children.

Children naturally imitate things around them and these exercises will stimulate their imaginations along with enhancing physical and neurological skills. First looking at a photo of the animal or object, children then enjoy learning how to make their bodies look like what they've seen. These poses will teach children how to stretch and strengthen every part of their body—even those that might not be reached in everyday activities.

Practicing yoga builds a strong foundation for children to grow from in order to become self-assured, clear-thinking, responsible people in the world. The poses strengthen and stretch the body, build coordination and skill, stimulate nerves and glands, and tone internal organs. Yoga teaches flexibility of the mind and the body. Staying flexible mentally by opening the mind fosters positive thinking and motivation to learn new things. The balance poses enhance concentration skills, which require focus and clarity of the mind. These mental skills enable children to learn more easily both in school and outside of school. Yoga poses develop the strength, flexibility, and coordination skills that help to prevent injury during sports or other physical activities.

In passing along this information to parents, teachers, and children, the goal is to help everyone develop strong minds and bodies, and to learn to giggle and lighten up to release tension—which will keep the spirit bright and healthy. Children will enjoy the benefits of yoga for a full life ahead.

Some children are loose muscled and are more naturally flexible than others. However, experience shows that flexibility fades past the age of three in most children who do not bend and stretch regularly. It is amazing how many children cannot touch their toes with their legs straight. Flexibility can be learned at any age through practice.

Adults will enjoy helping a child or groups of children learn these poses, encouraging them to feel like the subject as they imitate a specific behavior or quality in a pose or game. Children need not be discouraged if some of these poses are too difficult at first. With regular practice the body will do surprising things!

You will notice some of the children in the photos are more flexible than others. There is always work to do on perfecting the poses, getting stronger and looser. That is the fun. Remember that the purpose of yoga is to help one better oneself, so encourage the children not to compare themselves to others. Everyone has different limitations and areas to work through. Always praise what is accomplished with practice, and *make sure children never force their bodies to do anything too difficult. Make sure they practice slowly without pushing too far.*

Before helping children with yoga practice, make sure they understand the reminders and guidelines on the next page:

10

Things to Remember
About Doing Yoga

After practicing a pose, take a moment to look at the picture or close your eyes and imagine the animal or object in the pose you imitated. Then imagine yourself beside the subject in the same pose. Do you look similar? Imagine your body imitating the animal or object. This will help you understand how you want to look in the pose.

As with any type of exercise, there are guidelines to follow. If you concentrate on each and every movement, and slowly move in and out of the pose, these poses are safe and fun.

Guidelines

◆ Do not eat for at least one hour before practice.
◆ Keep your feet bare to prevent slipping.
◆ To prevent injury, move slowly and concentrate as you go in and out of every pose.
◆ Get to know your weaknesses and build a strong, healthy body and mind through constant practice.
◆ Have fun!

Breathing and Relaxing

Balloon Tummy to Chest Breathing

(DEEP BREATHING)

This is a good way to breathe while you hold your yoga poses. Think of this…when you begin to blow up a balloon, you blow through the opening. The air slowly fills the top of the balloon. Then you let the air out. You let it move back down slowly until the balloon is empty and flat.

Sit or stand and pretend you have a balloon in your body. The opening of the balloon starts down in your belly and the top is near the top of your chest. When you inhale or breathe in deeply, feel the air fill your balloon up to the top. When you breathe out slowly, imagine the air moving back down the balloon to your belly.

When you practice your full balloon breathing slowly, think of a color for your balloon so it is easier to picture. It takes practice to breathe deeply, so keep trying. Try five breaths at first and then work up to more as your lungs get stronger. It is a great way to release tension from your body and mind by bringing oxygen to the brain. It helps you loosen up more as you practice yoga poses.

Balloon Tummy Breathing
(ABDOMINAL BREATHING)

This is a calming, relaxing breathing practice. Lie down on your back and relax your body, keeping your arms to your sides, palms up, legs open. Imagine a round balloon in your belly and pick a color for this balloon so it is easy to see in your mind.

When you inhale or breathe in, imagine the balloon filling up as your tummy rises up slowly toward the sky (without pushing it up). Then when you breathe out slowly, watch the balloon empty and feel your tummy flatten softly. Do not force this breath, let it happen slowly and naturally. Try five breaths at first, or more. See how you feel...Relaxed?

Breathing abdominally while you imagine a balloon in your belly is a quick way to calm and relax your body and mind. You are working on relaxing through the center, which sends that message to your head and down through your feet.

Floating on a Cloud

(RELAXATION)

(After yoga practice a parent or teacher
will talk the child through this visualization)

Place your head down to keep your neck in a straight line down to the base of your spine. Relax your face and relax behind your eyes, keeping your mouth quiet. Keep your legs open slightly with your feet falling out to the sides. See if you can feel your whole body melting. By now you are very relaxed.

Now, imagine a cloud floating down to the ground toward you. Without moving a muscle, see yourself climbing onto that cloud and floating up in the sky. This is a very full, fluffy cloud, and you are feeling very cozy and comfortable on it like you are resting on a big overstuffed pillow.

Look at the colors around you as you float among many other clouds of different shapes and sizes. Notice how light your body feels as you float and enjoy the ride, feeling peaceful and happy.

Watch your cloud move down slowly through the sky toward the ground. Once it meets the earth, see yourself climbing off carefully and moving your muscles to get off the cloud. Notice and feel your body on the ground; you are still lying down, but see if you feel heavier now. Take a deep breath and stretch your arms and legs slowly, then stretch your face.

Bend your knees into your chest and roll your whole body over onto your left side to rest for a moment. Then roll over to the right. Rise up slowly to a sitting position with the legs crossed and your back straight. Take a deep breath. Don't you feel great?

To the parent or teacher: This guided visualization can last as long as three minutes or less, depending on the age of the children and their attention span. Children ages 3 to 6 will not be able to do it for very long, but give them enough time to keep every muscle relaxed, without moving any part of the body before you end. It is tough for young children to understand how to relax their muscles, so they need to work up to it slowly.

CHAPTER ONE

Nature's World

Mountain Pose

Mountains rise high toward the sky. Some are covered with trees and others look like giant rocks. When you think of a mountain, imagine something that is solid and won't fall down.

HOW TO DO THE MOUNTAIN POSE:

Stand tall with feet together, arms down at your sides. Point your fingers straight down toward the ground to draw your shoulders down away from your ears.

At first you will tip from side to side, so keep balancing your weight evenly through both feet, planting yourself into the earth. Close your eyes, and stand tall, with the top of your head lifted up toward the sky. Plant your feet into the earth with your legs straight. Breathe deeply while you do this.

Have someone time you while you hold the pose for one minute, concentrating with your eyes closed. Have someone tap your shoulder while you try not to move at all.

Benefits: This is a basic alignment pose to learn how to hold the body correctly for good posture. It strengthens the mind by developing concentration.

Tree
Pose

A tree has roots that grow down below the earth and a trunk and branches that grow up toward the sky.

HOW TO DO THE TREE POSE:

Stand in the Mountain Pose until you are steady. Look at one spot on the ground or floor in front of you.

Without moving your left foot, bring your right foot up as high as you can against your left inner leg.

Open your right knee out to the side and push your right
foot into your inner thigh so it doesn't slip down. The
open knee is your low branch. Keep your left leg straight
for the tree trunk. Bring both arms out to the sides like
medium-high branches. If you are balanced, you can
inhale and raise your arms up overhead with your
palms together to make high branches.

Concentrate and breathe deeply while someone
counts to ten or more. Release your arms slowly, then
your right leg, standing back in Mountain Pose before
you repeat on the other side.

Benefits: This pose strengthens the abdominals, hips, legs, and ankles, as well as
the mind. It teaches balance and concentration. It stretches the arms and chest.

Star
Pose

Stars are very far away and seem to twinkle. They look as if they had different points or edges.

HOW TO DO THE STAR POSE:
Sit down and put the soles of your feet together in front to make a diamond shape with your legs. Lace your fingers together and place your hands behind your head. Now slowly move your head down toward your feet.

This will take practice, but eventually you will be able to put your head on your feet. Have someone count the points of your star by looking at edges like elbows, knees, head and feet.

Breathe deeply and feel your back grow longer before you bring your head down further, while someone counts to ten or more. Then rise slowly to release.

Benefits: This pose stretches the arms, back, hips, and ankles. It also brings blood to the head to clear the mind.

Flower Pose

Flowers come in all colors, shapes, and sizes. The delicate petals of the iris are velvety soft, opening gracefully to display their beauty.

HOW TO DO THE FLOWER POSE:
Sit down, bend your knees, and pull your feet close to your body. Bring one arm at a time in between your legs, under the back of each bent knee. Bring the soles of your feet together so your legs make a diamond in the air.

Hold the middle finger and index finger together with the hands away from the shins. Now try to straighten your back by lifting your chest high. Look up to concentrate while breathing deeply. Hold the pose while someone counts to ten or more.

When you have practiced the pose several times, close your eyes and try to hold the pose. Slowly release your arms first and then your legs.

Benefits: This pose stretches shoulders, arms, and hips. It strengthens the mind, abdominal muscles, and back.

Crooked Branch Pose

A branch can extend out in any direction from the trunk of a tree. Take a look outside and notice how every branch bends differently, and most are crooked!

HOW TO DO THE CROOKED BRANCH POSE:

Lie down on your back with your body straight, arms to the sides, and legs together. Bend your knees and bring your feet flat on the ground toward your seat.

Now move both bent legs to the right side all the way to the ground, keeping your knees together and your feet back toward your seat. Your spine is twisted to make a crooked branch. Keep both shoulders down on the ground and look over your left shoulder to stretch your neck. Hold the pose, breathing deeply, while someone counts to ten or more. Straighten out and repeat to the other side.

Benefits: This pose tones the digestive organs, strengthens the back and stretches the neck, shoulders, and hips.

Rainbow
Pose

Bright ribbons of red, orange, yellow, green, blue, and violet arch across the sky when the sun shines through rain clouds.

HOW TO DO THE RAINBOW POSE:

Lie down on your right side, with your right hand under your shoulder, arm straight, and fingers out to the side. With your body in a straight line and your left hand on the ground in front, push down through both hands and feet to lift your right hip up from the ground.

Keep your legs tight and straight to balance on your right hand and the side of your right foot, with your left foot on top. Now try to lift your left arm up toward the sky. Have someone count to ten as you hold the pose and breathe deeply. Come down slowly and repeat to the other side.

Benefits: This pose strengthens the arms, back, and legs. It teaches balance and concentration.

Group Cactus Pose

Cactus plants live in dry desert climates because they don't need much water. They protect themselves with sharp thorns, and some of them grow into unusual shapes.

HOW TO DO THE GROUP CACTUS POSE:

Have a parent or teacher play some fun music with a group of your friends or classmates. Begin by standing tall.

Each person begins to dance around to the music, and listens carefully. When the music stops, stop moving and form your own cactus with crooked arms and legs. Balance any way you like.

The parent or teacher will watch to see who the last person is to stop moving, and that person will leave the group. The last person left wins the game.

Group Flower Pose

These tulips open when the sun comes out and close up again when it gets dark at night.

HOW TO DO THE GROUP FLOWER POSE:
Pick a captain to direct the group. Sit down in a circle close together with at least three friends. Each person will bend their knees and bring their arms in between their legs under the back of each knee in the Flower Pose.

Sit close enough so you will be able to hold
each neighbor's hand to close the circle. This is
difficult. You each need to balance in your flower
pose so you won't pull each other down. Keep
your feet together until everyone is balanced.

When everyone is ready and balanced, the captain
will ask you to go further and straighten both legs
out and open to the sides crossing your neighbor's
legs without falling over. Hold the pose while the
captain counts to ten or more. The captain will
say when to slowly release your arms first and
then your legs. Wow, that is hard work!

Group Yucca Pose

A yucca has stiff, evergreen, sword-shaped leaves. Its tall stalk rises up from the center like a candle with flowers that look like pods.

HOW TO DO THE GROUP YUCCA POSE:
You will need at least four friends for this group pose. Sit down in a circle far apart so every person can spread legs wide open on the ground with the sole of each foot touching the neighbor to either side. Try to keep your legs straight with the back of each leg down.

Now each person will bring their arms in between their open legs, trying to stretch forward and down in front without lifting the back of the legs. The circle of friends will hold this stretch.

One or more will stand in the middle of the circle with feet flat on the ground, hip width apart. Keeping the legs straight, the center people will bring their hands against their seat and bend back breathing and holding the pose.

Hold the pose while someone counts to ten or more. Then roll up slowly to straighten your back, release your legs, and shake them out. Take turns being in the middle for the backbend pose.

CHAPTER TWO

All Kinds of Birds

Roadrunner Pose

With his strong legs and long tail, the roadrunner is built for running fast, but you'll rarely see him fly.

HOW TO DO THE ROADRUNNER POSE:

Start on your hands and knees with your back straight. Your hands are placed under your shoulders with palms flat on the ground, fingers wide and pointing forward. Your knees are under your hips. The tops of your feet are on the ground, with toes pointing back.

Bring your left foot up between your hands, bending your knee over your heel at a right angle. Straighten your right leg out behind you, curling the toes under to lift your leg from the ground, and push back through the heel. Hold the pose, breathing deeply, while someone counts to ten or more.

Bring your right knee to the ground under your hip. Then slide your left foot back so you are on hands and knees again. Repeat to the other side.

Benefits: This pose stretches the front of the legs and hips, and the back.

Pigeon Pose

Pigeons come to towns and cities because they like to roost on the roofs of tall buildings. And where people live, pigeons can usually find something to eat.

HOW TO DO PIGEON POSE I:

Start on hands and knees in the same beginning stance as the Roadrunner Pose. Slide your right knee as far forward in front of your right hip as you can. Bring your right shin to the ground and angle your foot over in front of your left hip, toes pointing back.

Then slide your left leg straight back behind you, with your toes pointing back. Keep the front of your left leg and foot down to the ground. Move your palms back toward your hips on the ground to lift up your chest and feel your lower back bending. Relax your shoulders down away from your ears.

Breathe deeply and hold the pose while someone counts to ten or more. Then, slide your right knee to the ground under your hip. Pull your left knee forward until you are on hands and knees again. Repeat to the other side.

Benefits: This pose stretches the chest, belly, hips, and legs. It also strengthens the lower back.

HOW TO DO PIGEON POSE II:

Start on hands and knees. Slide your right leg in front with your knee bent. Slide your left leg straight back as you did in Pigeon Pose I.

Then walk your hands out in front as far as you can to bring your arms, head, and chest to the ground.

Breathe deeply and hold the pose while someone counts to ten or more. Then, walk your hands back to straighten your arms and lift your chest up. Slide your right knee back to the ground under your hip. Pull your left knee forward until you are on hands and knees again. Repeat to the other side.

Benefits: This pose stretches the arms, back, hips, and legs.

Eagles glide high in the air on broad wings. With their powerful eyesight they can spot their prey—small animals and birds far below.

Eagle Pose

HOW TO DO THE EAGLE POSE:

Stand in Mountain Pose with feet together. Bring both arms out in front of your chest, palms facing down. Cross your right arm over your left, keeping your right elbow above your left. Bend your elbows and put the backs of your hands together like a beak, fingers pointing up. Place your right hand on your forehead.

Look through your hands with your sharp eyes to focus on the ground in front of you. Bend both knees and cross your right leg around the front of your left and point the toes of your right foot to the ground. Keep your left foot flat on the ground for balance.

When you are balancing well you can try to bring the right foot up to the outside of the left knee. Hold the pose, breathing deeply, and have someone count to ten or more. Release your right leg, then bring your arms down to your sides in the Mountain Pose. Repeat to the other side. (You can also do it with arms and legs opposite, like this girl.)

Benefits: This pose stretches the upper back, shoulders, and wrists. It strengthens the mind, legs, and ankles, and improves balance.

41

Ostrich Pose

The ostrich is the largest of all living birds. He runs very fast but does not fly. He does not hide his head in the sand when afraid, as people think. But with his long neck, he can dip his head way down to eat.

HOW TO DO THE OSTRICH POSE:

Start on hands and knees with your hands under your shoulders, palms flat, fingers wide and turned in to the center. Your knees are together, under your hips, with your feet lifted up.

Keep your back straight and bend your elbows. Move your chest forward. Keep your chest and head in front of your hands and above the ground.

Hold the pose, breathe deeply, while someone counts to ten or more. Sit back on your heels to release. Repeat.

Benefits: This pose strengthens the arms, wrists, and back.

Bird Walk Race

Birds walk in different ways. These black skimmers hurry along the edge of the water looking for something to eat.

HOW TO DO THE BIRD WALK RACE: Line up side by side with two or more friends. Squat down with knees spread wide apart. Bring your arms in between your legs, if you can open your knees that wide, to hold each ankle in front, as this girl is doing. (This will get easier as you practice.)

44

Have a parent or teacher stand a
good distance away in front to mark
a finish line. The leader says "Start"
to begin the race.

To walk like a bird, you must
hold your ankles and lift up one foot
at a time and walk fast. The first bird
to the finish line wins!

CHAPTER THREE

Four-Legged Animals

Cat Pose

Cats are very good at yoga stretches. This one arches his back up in the air to stretch out after a nap.

HOW TO DO THE CAT POSE:

Start on hands and knees. Keep your hands under
your shoulders, palms flat, fingers wide and
forward, your knees under your hips, shins on
the ground, and toes pointing back.

Take a deep breath. When you exhale, tighten your
tummy muscles and arch your back up toward the sky.
Hold the pose with your breath flowing easily.
Have someone count to ten. Release and repeat five times.

Benefits: This pose strengthens the abdominal muscles and stretches the back.

Rabbit
Pose

Rabbits stay low to the ground
when they sniff around looking
for something to eat.

Start on hands and knees the way
you started the Cat Pose.

Place the top of your head flat on the ground and stretch your back up as high as you can.

Lock your fingers together behind your back and pull your arms straight up. Hold the pose as long as you can, breathing deeply, while someone counts. Bring your forehead down, release your hands, and roll up slowly with your back straight.

Benefits: This pose stretches the shoulders, arms and back. It strengthens the legs and clears the mind as the blood moves into the head.

Coyote Pose

A coyote is a wild dog who looks like a wolf but is smaller. He raises his head to howl at night.

HOW TO DO THE COYOTE POSE:

Sit on your heels with your toes curled under and knees on the ground. Turn your fingers in toward your knees with palms flat on the ground and little fingers together. Relax your shoulders away from your ears to open your chest.

Keep your arms straight and lift your chest. Stretch up through your chin and howl to the wind. Hold the pose, breathing deeply, while someone counts to ten or more. Release and stretch your legs and toes out.

Benefits: This pose stretches the chin, chest, arms, wrists, and toes. It also strengthens the back.

Dog
Pose

Watch how dogs stretch
their back and legs out when
they get up from resting.

HOW TO DO THE DOG POSE:

Start on hands and knees the way you
started the Cat Pose. Keep your back
long, and bring your toes under to lift
your knees from the ground.

Straighten your arms and legs so your body
is in a "V" position. Press your heels down.
Breathe deeply and have someone count to
ten or more. Come down on hands and
knees to release.

Benefits: This pose is wonderful for stretching and strengthening the arms,
back, and legs. It clears your mind by bringing more blood to your head.

Beaver Pose

Beavers make ponds by building dams over streams out of trees and branches. In the winter, a beaver family spends most of its time in a snug home inside the dam.

HOW TO DO THE BEAVER POSE:

Sit down on your right hip with your knees together and bent to the left, feet pointing back.

Place your left hand flat down beside your right knee and your right hand under your right shoulder. Fingers of both hands are pointing forward, palms down. Your two hands and your knees will be in a straight line.

Bend your elbows to push your chest forward, keeping your head above the ground in front of your hands. Breathe deeply and hold the pose while someone counts to ten or more. Then change sides and repeat.

Benefits: This pose strengthens the shoulders, arms, upper back, and wrists.

Donkey Kick Pose

A donkey is a strong animal related to the horse. He works like a horse, carrying things and pulling things around. If he gets mad, he will kick up his hind legs and hee-haw!

HOW TO DO THE DONKEY KICK POSE:

Stand facing a wall and place your palms flat on the ground a foot from the wall and under your shoulders, fingers wide and forward.

Keep your head in the air and look in front of your hands. Push your chest forward to kick your feet up in the air one at a time, bending your knees and arching your lower back. Kick ten times, then rest.

As you get stronger you will be able to touch the wall kicking up both feet with your knees bent.
Feel your heart beating fast?

Benefits: This active pose strengthens the back, arms, wrists, and heart. It clears the mind by bringing the blood to the head.

Dog
Walk
Race

HOW TO DO THE DOG WALK RACE:
Two or more friends line up side by side
starting in the Dog Pose.

Have a parent or teacher stand a good distance away in front of the group to mark a finish line. The leader says "Start" to begin the race. To walk like a dog, you must keep arms and legs straight. Walk fast moving your right hand and right foot forward. Then your left hand and left foot follow.

The first dog to the finish line wins!

Bunny Hop Race

This angora rabbit has long silky fur that can be combed out to make soft yarn.

HOW TO DO THE BUNNY HOP RACE:
Line up standing side by side with two or more friends. Place a big ball between your legs. Bend your knees to squeeze the ball and hold it in place. Bend your arms and hands near your chest like the front paws of a rabbit.

Have a parent or teacher stand a good
distance away in front to mark a finish
line. The leader says "Start" to begin the
race. Hop straight ahead like a bunny,
while you hold the ball between your
legs. What a workout! Good luck.

CHAPTER FOUR

Things That Move

Windmill Pose

When the wind blows, the windmill turns. It catches the wind to produce electric power or to pump water. Many years ago it was used to grind wheat into flour.

HOW TO DO THE WINDMILL POSE:

Stand with your legs wide, feet flat on the floor, keeping legs straight and feet forward.

Stretch forward and bring your left palm to the ground in between your legs, fingers pointing to the right foot. Swing your right arm up toward the sky with the palm facing forward. Feel the twist in your spine and look up at your fingers in the air.

Hold the pose and breathe deeply while someone counts to ten or more. Then change hands. After you hold the other side for the same count, roll your back up slowly to your standing position. Bring your feet together in Mountain Pose.

Benefits: This pose strengthens the back and stretches the arms, wrists, and legs. It also clears the mind by bringing blood into the head.

Gate Pose

A gate opens and closes to let you in and out. When the gate is closed you may have to stand tall and peek to see what's inside.

HOW TO DO THE GATE POSE:

Kneel with both knees under your hips, the tops of your feet on the ground and toes pointing back. Bring your right leg out to the side with the heel down and toes up. Place your right hand on your right leg, keeping it straight.

Look up over your left shoulder and raise your left arm up toward the sky. Reach over your head, and over your right leg. Keep your left elbow behind your ear, and your palm facing down. Try to slide your right hand down your leg to stretch further. Breathe deeply and keep your chest open.

As you practice, your arm will stretch further over your leg and you will try to put your toes on the ground. Hold the pose, and have someone count to ten or more. Straighten up, release your left arm, and change sides.

Benefits: This pose stretches the arms and waist and strengthens the hips and legs.

Boat
Pose

A canoe is a boat with a curved bottom. It can be paddled down rapids or across peaceful lakes. This Bolivian canoe is made out of reeds that grow by the lake.

HOW TO DO THE FRONT BOAT POSE:
Lie down on your tummy and keep your legs straight and together, arms to your sides, chin to the ground.

Take a deep breath. As you exhale, reach back with your arms to raise your chest, with your head up. Keep looking forward. Now raise straight legs up from the ground and hold the pose, while someone counts to ten or more. Release slowly, and take a deep breath. Repeat.

Benefits: This pose strengthens the back, and stretches the chest, arms, and legs.

HOW TO DO THE BACK BOAT POSE: Lie down on your back. Keep your legs straight and together, arms to the sides. Lift your head and tuck your chin to your chest. Lift your arms and reach out in front. Now lift your legs, keeping them straight. Keep your lower back on the ground. Flex your feet, toes up. Hold the pose, breathing deeply, while someone counts to ten or more. Come down, and take a deep breath. Repeat.

Benefits: This pose strengthens the abdominal muscles and front of the body.

Wheel Pose

Wheels are attached to wagons, carts, cars, tables, chairs, and all kinds of things to make them move. Notice how many interesting objects have wheels.

HOW TO DO THE WHEEL POSE (AGES 3 TO 6):

Sit down with your knees bent, feet hip width apart and flat on the ground away from your seat.

Place your palms down under your shoulders with fingers wide, pointing toward your knees.

Now lift your seat up high to stretch the front of your spine. Straighten your arms, and bring your head back. Hold the pose, breathing deeply, while someone counts to ten or more. Sit down slowly. Repeat three times. Do you feel that stretch in your tummy?

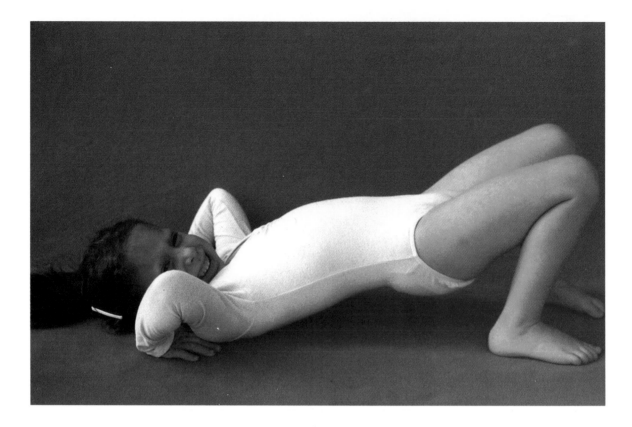

HOW TO DO THE WHEEL POSE (AGES 6 TO 12):

Lie down on your back with knees bent, feet pulled in flat toward your seat, hip width apart, toes forward. Bend your elbows and turn your hands under your shoulders to the ground, palms flat, fingers wide and pointing toward your feet.

Lift your belly and push down through your hands and feet to bring your body and head up, bending your back in a half-circle. Hold the pose, breathing deeply, while someone counts to five first, then longer after you've practiced and you get stronger. Come down slowly and take a deep breath.

This is very hard to do. Do you feel your heart beating fast? Try three times.

Benefits: Both of these poses strengthen the arms and back, stretch the front spine and legs, and clear the mind by bringing the blood to the head.

Plow Pose

An old-fashioned plow is wooden and is pushed to loosen the dirt for seed planting. Modern plows are attached to the front of a tractor. Some plows can be lifted up, turned upside down to scoop up dirt or snow and move it from one place to another.

HOW TO DO THE PLOW POSE:

Lie down on your back with arms to your sides, knees into your chest.

Swing your legs up and over your head, keeping them straight, toes down, while you straighten your back by lifting your seat up toward the sky. Look straight up and keep your arms on the ground or use them to hold your back up. Hold and breathe deeply while someone counts to ten or more.

Roll your back down slowly with your seat to the ground and your legs up to the sky. Keep your legs straight, toes up, and slowly lower them to the ground with your back down. Do you feel your heart beating fast? Take a deep breath.

Benefits: This pose stretches the arms and back, strengthens the heart and tones the thyroid. It also clears the mind.

Car
Pose

There are so many makes and models of cars, but the basics are the same...every car has a body, a steering wheel, four wheels, and at least two seats in front—and you need a key to turn on the engine.

HOW TO DO THE CAR POSE:

Sit down with your legs together straight out in front, toes up. Bring your arms in front of your chest and pretend you are holding a steering wheel to drive your car.

Start your own engine—rrrr rrrr rrrr! To move forward, scoot your hips back and forth and keep your legs straight. Move your arms to hold your steering wheel as you drive. You can practice turning your body to the right, or left, in circles or drive backwards. Have fun and feel your hips working away!

HOW TO DO THE CAR RACE:

You need at least two people for this race. Line up side by side in your Car Pose. Have a parent or teacher stand a good distance away in front to mark a finish line. The leader says "Start" and the race begins. You can race backwards too. Good luck!

Benefits: This active pose strengthens the legs and back and keeps the hips and shoulders loose.

Wheelbarrow Race

You would be amazed at how many different things you can carry around in a wheelbarrow...you can even give your dog or cat a ride!

HOW TO DO THE WHEELBARROW RACE:

You need at least four people for this race. Two or more people line up side by side standing. A partner starts on hands and knees close in front of each standing person.

The person on the ground will straighten and lift one leg back at a time. The standing partner holds the partner's ankles in the air. It takes great upper body strength for the bottom person to walk with arms, back, and legs straight.

Have a parent or teacher stand a good distance away in front to mark a finish line. The leader says "Start" to begin the race. The standing person will guide the wheelbarrow in a straight line down to the finish line. The strongest and fastest team will win.

Partners can reverse positions and try again. Good Luck!

CHAPTER FIVE

Things That Stay Still

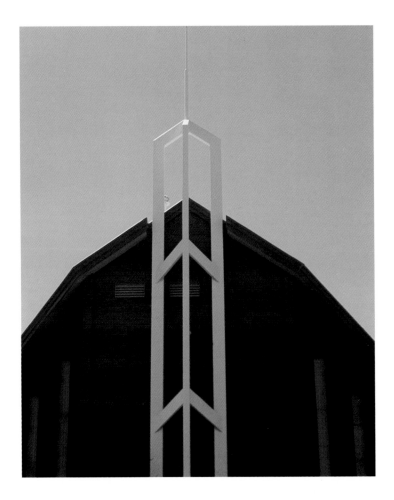

Steeple Pose

A steeple rises up high on top of a church building, pointing to the heavens.

HOW TO DO THE STEEPLE POSE:

Stand in the Mountain Pose. Inhale and raise your arms up overhead, palms together with your elbows back behind your ears.

Keep your legs and arms straight and stretch to the right with your chest forward. Try to stretch further over as you hold the pose, breathing deeply. Have someone count to ten or more. Come back to the Mountain Pose and change sides.

Benefits: This pose stretches the shoulders, arms, and waist.

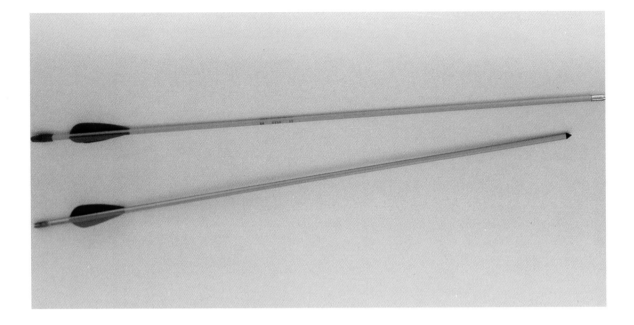

Arrow Pose

An arrow has a point on one end and a feathered weight on the other end to give it balance as it flies through the air.

HOW TO DO THE ARROW POSE:
Stand with your legs wide apart, turning your right foot out to the side and your left foot in toward the right.

Bring your chest over your right leg and bend your
right knee over your right heel. Lower your chest
over your thigh, keeping your back straight, and
stretch your arms out in front, palms together,
pointing your fingers straight out like an arrow. Your
left leg stays straight, pushing down through the heel.

Hold the pose, breathing deeply, while
someone counts to ten or more.

Lift your chest up, release your arms down,
straighten your right leg, and repeat to the other
side. Do you feel how strong that makes your legs?

Benefits: This pose stretches the shoulders, arms, and back. It strengthens the legs, hips, and ankles.

Bridge Pose

Bridges are built over rivers, canyons, and highways. They have to be very strong in order to carry trains, cars, and trucks.

HOW TO DO THE BRIDGE POSE:

Lie down on your back with your knees bent and your feet flat on the ground hip width apart, close to your seat, and arms down at your sides.

Now begin lifting your lower spine from the ground, slowly moving up 'til you get to the shoulders. With your arms down straight, lock your fingers, as you stretch the front of your spine and legs.

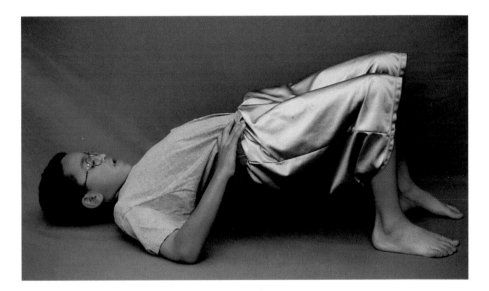

If you want to stretch further, bend your elbows and hold your waist with your thumbs and fingers.

Hold the pose, breathing deeply, while someone counts to ten or more. Roll your back down slowly from your shoulders and take a deep breath. Repeat.

Benefits: This pose strengthens the back and seat. It stretches the front of the body and opens the lungs.

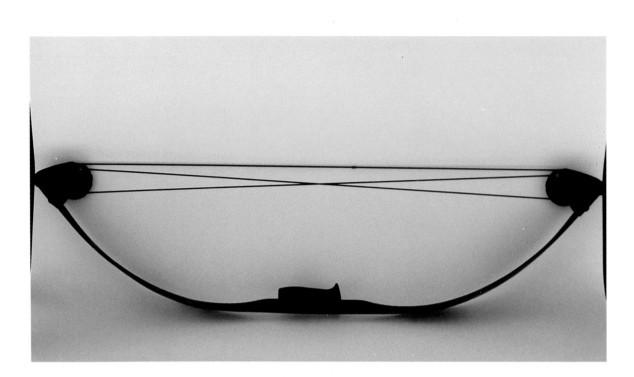

Bow
Pose

When you pull the bow string, the bow arches into a half circle, ready to shoot an arrow off into the distance.

HOW TO DO THE BOW POSE:
Lie down on your tummy with your arms to your sides, chin to the ground.

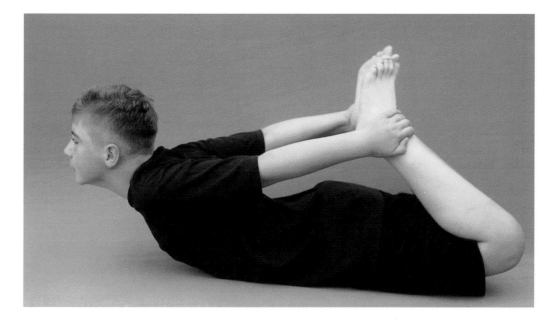

Bend your knees and bring your feet up toward your seat. Take a deep breath, exhale and lift your chest from the ground, as you reach your hands back like the bow string to hold your feet.

Try to lift your thighs from the ground to curve your back into a bow. Hold the pose, breathing deeply, while someone counts to ten or more. Roll down slowly and take a deep breath. Repeat.

Benefits: This pose strengthens the back and stretches the shoulders, arms, and front of the body.

Slide Pose

When you sit down at the top of a slide, be ready to shoot down fast until you hit the ground at the bottom.

HOW TO DO THE SLIDE POSE:
Sit down with your legs together, straight out in front, toes up.

Bring your hands under your shoulders, palms flat, fingers pointing toward your feet. Keeping your legs straight, and your seat tight, push your feet down and lift your tummy up as high as you can to straighten your arms. Make sure your weight is balanced between your hands and feet.

Hold the pose, breathing deeply, while someone counts to ten or more. Come down slowly and take a deep breath. Repeat.

Benefits: This pose strengthens the shoulders, arms, wrists, back and legs. It stretches the chest and front body.

Candle Pose

A candle needs to stand straight when the wick is lit or the melting wax will all dribble down one side.

HOW TO DO THE CANDLE POSE:
Lie down on your back with your knees into your chest, arms to your sides.

Now swing your hips up, bending your elbows to hold your back up with your hands while keeping your upper arms and shoulders on the ground. Try to straighten your back and lift your legs up straight toward the sky, toes up. A parent or teacher can lift your legs higher. Your toes are the wick.

Hold the pose, breathing deeply, while someone counts to ten or more. Lower your legs over your head and roll your back down slowly, bringing your seat down, legs straight up. Now lower your legs to the ground slowly, and take a deep breath. Wow, that feels great! Repeat.

Benefits: This pose is good for relieving headaches, and helping colds by opening sinus passageways. It also strengthens the heart, back, and arms.

Group Staircase Pose

A staircase can go up in a straight line or spiral or turn this way and that. Whichever way the stairs go, if you go up, you must come down!

HOW TO DO THE GROUP STAIRCASE POSE:

You need at least three people for this pose and a parent or teacher to help everyone get in position.

One person will lie down on his back keeping legs straight, arms to the sides. The second person will put her head on the tummy of the first person and lie on her back, body out to the side of the first person at a right angle. The third person will put his head on the tummy of the second person, body straight out to the side at a right angle.

You can add more and more people. Now laugh hard and feel the tummy under your head moving up and down and jiggling like jello!

Group Bridge Pose

HOW TO DO THE GROUP BRIDGE POSE:

You need at least two people for this pose. With more than two, you can create a circle.

Lie down on your backs in a circle with heads toward the center in the Bridge Pose starting position. Make sure you have enough room to reach your arms out straight and above your head to hold your neighbor's hands.

Have a parent or teacher say when to rise
up slowly lifting the seat up in the air,
keeping arms overhead. Hold the pose,
breathing deeply, while the adult counts
to ten or more and tells everyone to roll
down slowly, holding hands.

CHAPTER SIX

Desert Creatures

Rattlesnake Pose

The rattlesnake has a set of hard jointed rings at the end of its tail that it vibrates to make a rattling noise to warn you to stay away. This is the most dangerous poisonous snake in the United States. If you see one coiled, with its head up—watch out—it's ready to strike!

HOW TO DO THE RATTLESNAKE POSE:

Lie down on your tummy with your legs together and straight. Bring your hands under your shoulders, palms down, fingers wide and forward, chin on the ground.

Push your hands down and begin lifting your chest up slowly, rising up as high as you can, until you straighten your arms. Hold your head back and stretch your throat. Lift your feet from the ground for the rattle.

Hold the pose, breathing deeply, while someone counts to ten or more. Put your feet down and roll your spine down slowly, bending your elbows. Take a deep breath and repeat.

Benefits: This pose stretches the front spine, throat, chest, and shoulders. It strengthens the back and tones the kidneys.

Scorpion Pose

Scorpions have been around for a long time—they are believed to be the first land creatures. The scorpion has a poisonous sting on the end of its tail. With its tail curled over its back, it's ready to strike insects, spiders, other small animals—or anything that comes along. Watch out if you see one, they are not friendly!

HOW TO DO THE SCORPION POSE:

Start on hands and knees and bring your forearms down to the ground, elbows under your shoulders, palms down, thumbs open wide and fingers forward. Hold your head off the ground. Knees are together under your hips with your spine long, toes under.

Lift your knees off the ground and straighten your legs, pressing your heels down toward the ground. Lift your right leg up in the air, bending your knee to make a tail. Hold the pose, breathing deeply, while someone counts to ten or more. Bring the right leg down and lift the left leg. Come down and rest, sitting back on your heels with your forehead to the ground, arms to your sides.

Benefits: This pose strengthens the wrists, arms, shoulders, and back. It stretches the bottom leg and heel, and brings blood to the head which helps to clear the mind.

Spider Pose

This furry spider from East Africa is ready for a fight. There are 40,000 different kinds of spiders, and all of them have eight legs. It is a good idea to watch them from a distance because some of them are poisonous.

HOW TO DO THE SPIDER POSE:

Lie down on your back, knees bent into your chest, arms down at your sides.

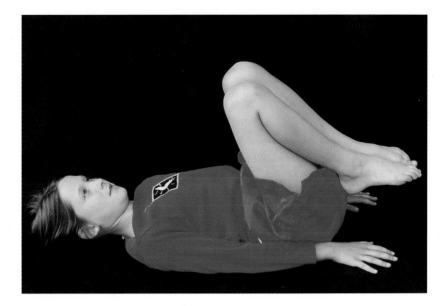

Swing your hips up from the ground and hold your back up with your hands, legs straight overhead, toes toward the ground. Keep your shoulders and upper arms on the ground. Bend your knees toward the ground to press your ears; eventually your toes will rest back over your head on the ground.

Hold the pose, breathing deeply, while someone counts to ten or more. Roll your back down slowly until your seat is on the ground, keeping legs straight to the sky. Keep your back down and lower your straight legs to the ground slowly. Take a deep breath.

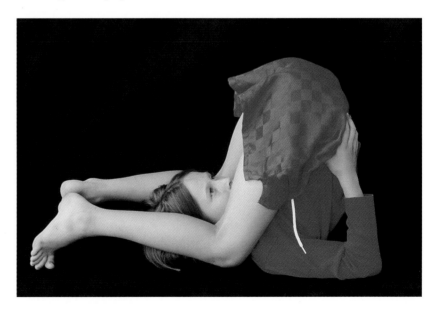

Benefits: This pose relieves headaches, and stretches the shoulders, arms, neck, hips and back. It strengthens the abdominal muscles.

Lizard Pose

Lizards are scaly reptiles related to snakes and dinosaurs. There are about 3,000 kinds of lizards, including geckos, chameleons, and gila monsters. This iguana is sunning himself beside a swimming pool.

HOW TO DO THE LIZARD POSE:
Lie down on your belly with legs together and straight. Curl your toes under, feet hip width apart, palms flat down under your shoulders, fingers forward, chin down.

Now try to lift your legs up from the
ground, pushing down through your toes.

Push down through your hands and see if you can lift your
chest too. Eventually you will be able to lift your head, looking
down. Your body will be in a straight line lifting from the ground
like a push-up. You can practice lifting one area at a time.
This is very hard to do, but don't give up. Just keep practicing.

Benefits: This pose strengthens the arms, shoulders, wrists, and back. It also stretches the toes.

Snake Race

These red garter snakes are not poisonous but they will protect themselves if they need to!

HOW TO DO THE SNAKE RACE:

You need at least two people for this race. Line up side by side in the Rattlesnake Pose, feet down.

Have a parent or teacher stand a good distance
away in front of the group to mark a finish line.
The leader will say "Start" and each person
will push down through the hands and "walk"
forward using the upper body, with hips and legs
straight and together. Slither as fast as you can
to the finish line hissing like a snake. Good Luck!

For Parents and Teachers

How to Get the Most out of This Book

The poses in each chapter are listed in order of difficulty, beginning with the easiest to practice. Each chapter contains a balanced array of poses to stretch and strengthen the entire body. The chapters are also listed in order of difficulty, beginning with easier poses to practice in Chapters one, two, and three and poses that work the body harder in Chapters four and five. Chapter six contains the most difficult poses.

The poses can be held at first counting to ten. As the child progressively gets stronger in a particular pose, the count will increase. Don't worry about holding a yoga pose too long—tell the children to let the body decide when it has had enough!

Many of the balance poses are frustrating for children at first because they are not skilled at concentrating. These are highly beneficial even though they take time to master. It is important to keep encouraging children to go on practicing the poses that are difficult for them. In time, when their bodies get stronger, these difficult poses take less effort, and they will feel proud of having accomplished this feat. This is an excellent way to build self-esteem.

Older children often enjoy helping younger children practice the poses in a group situation. They will also invent creative ways to explore poses together. Talk to the children and you will be amazed at how their imaginations spark new ideas of combining poses involving all ages in a fun way. An adult may need to supervise situations where poses are combined as a game, to prevent injuries. For instance, an older child could practice the advanced Wheel Pose while a small young child crawls under the wheel staying low like a snake.

The poses in this book can be practiced anywhere—indoors or outdoors. There is no special equipment needed except a ball for the Bunny Hop. Stay involved with maintaining a healthy balanced life for your children by practicing yoga with them. Adults will be amazed at how much fun and how challenging some of these poses can be. Don't delay—get moving and use this book today!

Poses to Relieve
Common Physical Ailments

Yoga is a healing art, designed to tone the internal organs and release stress. When a pose is held for a period of time, the blood pools into certain areas of the body to stimulate organs, tissues, and nerves, which relieves tension that causes stress. The poses listed below relieve some common physical problems children experience. Have the child hold the pose for one or two minutes when working on relieving stressful symptoms.

Headache: Star Pose, Rabbit Pose, Bridge Pose, Candle Pose, Plow Pose, Cloud Relaxation.

Lower Back Ache: Star Pose, Crooked Branch Pose, Cat Pose, Rabbit Pose, Spider Pose, Arrow Pose, Dog Pose.

Constipation: Flower Pose, Crooked Branch Pose, Cat Pose, Bird Walk Race, Spider Pose, Arrow Pose, Plow Pose, Back Boat Pose.

Colds or Sinus Problems: Star Pose, Dog Pose, Ostrich Pose, Scorpion Pose, Spider Pose, Candle Pose, Plow Pose, Wheel Pose.

Stomach Ache: Tree Pose, Dog Pose, Bridge Pose, Rattlesnake Pose, Wheel Pose.

Poses to Stretch or Strengthen Specific Areas

(In order as they appear in this book)

**UPPER BODY
STRETCHING POSES:**

(For Arms, Shoulders, and Wrists)

1. Tree Pose
2. Flower Pose
*3. Crooked Branch Pose
*4. Group Flower Pose
*5. Group Yucca Pose
6. Pigeon Pose I
7. Pigeon Pose II
8. Eagle Pose
9. Rabbit Pose
*10. Coyote Pose
11. Dog Pose
12. Windmill Pose
13. Gate Pose
14. Front Boat Pose
15. Wheel Pose
16. Plow Pose
17. Car Pose
18. Steeple Pose
*19. Arrow Pose
20. Bridge Pose
21. Bow Pose
22. Slide Pose
23. Rattlesnake Pose
24. Spider Pose

**LOWER BODY
STRETCHING POSES:**

(For Hips, Legs, and Toes)

1. Star Pose
2. Flower Pose
*3. Crooked Branch Pose
*4. Group Flower Pose
*5. Group Yucca Pose
6. Rabbit Pose
*7. Coyote Pose
8. Roadrunner Pose
9. Pigeon Pose I
10. Pigeon Pose II
*11. Ostrich Pose
12. Cat Pose
*13. Arrow Pose
*14. Scorpion Pose
15. Spider Pose

SIDE STRETCHING POSES:

*1. Crooked Branch Pose
2. Rainbow Pose
3. Windmill Pose
4. Gate Pose
5. Steeple Pose

*Poses created by the author

TWISTING POSES:

*1. Crooked Branch Pose
2. Windmill Pose

BACK STRETCHING POSES:

1. Star Pose
*2. Flower Pose
*3. Group Yucca Pose
4. Roadrunner Pose
5. Pigeon Pose II
6. Eagle Pose
7. Cat Pose
8. Rabbit Pose
9. Dog Pose
10. Back Boat Pose
11. Plow Pose
*12. Arrow Pose
13. Spider Pose

BACK STRENGTHENING POSES:

1. Flower Pose
*2. Crooked Branch Pose
*3. Group Yucca Pose (center person backbending)
4. Pigeon Pose I
5. Donkey Kick Pose
6. Windmill Pose
7. Front Boat Pose

8. Wheel Pose
9. Wheelbarrow Race
10. Bridge Pose
11. Bow Pose
12. Slide Pose
13. Candle Pose
*14. Group Bridge Pose
15. Rattlesnake Pose
*16. Scorpion Pose
17. Lizard Pose
18. Snake Race

UPPER BODY STRENGTHENING POSES:
(For Arms, Shoulders, and Wrists)

1. Rainbow Pose
*2. Group Yucca Pose
3. Pigeon Pose I
*4. Ostrich Pose
*5. Beaver Pose
*6. Dog Walk Race
7. Donkey Kick Pose
8. Wheel Pose
9. Plow Pose
10. Wheelbarrow Race
11. Slide Pose
12. Candle Pose
*13. Scorpion Pose
14. Lizard Pose
15. Snake Race

LOWER BODY STRENGTHENING POSES:
(For Leg, Hip, or Ankles)

1. Tree Pose
2. Rainbow Pose
3. Eagle Pose
*4. Bird Walk Race
5. Rabbit Pose
*6. Coyote Pose
7. Donkey Kick Pose
*8. Bunny Hop Race
9. Gate Pose
10. Back Boat Pose
11. Front Boat Pose
12. Wheel Pose
13. Car Pose
*14. Arrow Pose
15. Bridge Pose
16. Slide
17. Rattlesnake Pose
18. Lizard Pose

ABDOMINAL STRENGTHENING POSES:

1. Tree Pose
2. Star Pose
3. Flower Pose

*4. Group Flower Pose
*5. Group Yucca Pose
*6. Bird Walk Pose
7. Cat Pose
8. Rabbit Pose
9. Dog Pose
10. Gate Pose
11. Back Boat Pose
12. Plow Pose
13. Car Pose
14. Car Race
15. Steeple Pose
16. Spider Pose

BALANCE POSES FOR CONCENTRATION:

1. Mountain Pose
2. Tree Pose
3. Flower Pose
4. Rainbow Pose
*5. Group Cactus Pose
*6. Group Flower Pose
*7. Group Yucca Pose
8. Eagle Pose
9. Donkey Kick Pose
10. Wheelbarrow Pose

THIA LUBY, pictured above practicing yoga with her granddaughter, is an award-winning author and teacher. She was introduced to yoga at age sixteen by her older brother in 1972 and became an enthusiastic student. Her new passion led to intensive study of both the physical and the philosophical aspects of yoga and included work with nationally known teachers. In the process she developed her personalized style and created her own unique poses. In 1979, she became a mother, which sparked her interest in yoga for children and teens. Luby's daughter, Bianca, was raised on yoga and has helped teach children's classes. Luby now has two young grandchildren to educate and guide through a lifetime of yoga practice.

Luby's innovative programs for adults and teens are presented in her two other books, *Yoga of Nature* and *Yoga for Teens*, which received an honorable mention from *School Library Journal* and a great response from *Teen* magazine. She has been a columnist for the *Albuquerque Journal* as well as a contributor to a teen web site. Her adult audiotape and children's video on yoga are distributed nationally. After teaching yoga in Santa Fe, New Mexico, for over twenty years, Luby has recently opened a yoga center in Manitou Sprints, Colorado, where she now lives.

111